Math in My World

Math in the Neighborhood

By William Amato

Children's Press®
A Division of Scholastic Inc.
New York / Toronto / London / Auckland / Sydney
Mexico City / New Delhi / Hong Kong
Danbury, Connecticut

Photo Credits: Cover and all photos by Maura Boruchow

Contributing Editor: Jennifer Silate
Book Design: Laura Stein

Library of Congress Cataloging-in-Publication Data

Amato, William.
    Math in the neighborhood / by William Amato.
        p. cm. — (Math in my world)
    Includes bibliographical references and index.
    Summary: Photos and simple text illustrate counting windows, people, and cars on a walk to a friend's house.
        ISBN 0-516-23942-2 (lib. bdg.) — ISBN 0-516-23599-0 (pbk.)
        1. Mathematics—Juvenile literature. [1. Mathematics. 2. Counting.] I. Title.

    QA540.5 .A533 2002
    513.2'11—dc21

                                    2001042363

Contents

Dad is taking me to Tommy's house for **lunch**.

Tommy lives in our **neighborhood**.

Many different houses
are in our neighborhood.

This house has
many windows.

How many windows
does it have?

7

This house has five windows.

9

We have to cross the street.

How many cars are **parked** here?

Three cars are parked.

We are close to
Tommy's house.

Look, there is Carla
and her mom.

They are going to Tommy's house, too.

How many of us are going to Tommy's house?

Four of us are going to Tommy's house.

19

We are at Tommy's house.

It is time for lunch!

New Words

lunch (**luhnch**) a meal eaten in the middle of the day

neighborhood (**nay**-bur-hud) an area where a group of people live

parked (**parked**) when a car is left on a street or in a parking lot

To Find Out More

Books

MathArts: Exploring Math through Art for 3 to 6 Year Olds
by MaryAnn F. Kohl
Gryphon House

Pigs at Odds: Fun with Math and Games
by Amy Axelrod
Simon & Schuster Children's Press

Web Site

FunBrain.com—Numbers
http://www.funbrain.com/numbers.html
This site has many games that improve math skills.

Index

About the Author
William Amato is a teacher and writer living in New York City.

Reading Consultants
Kris Flynn, Coordinator, Small School District Literacy, The San Diego County Office of Education

Shelly Forys, Certified Reading Recovery Specialist, W.J. Zahnow Elementary School, Waterloo, IL

Sue McAdams, Former President of the North Texas Reading Council of the IRA, and Early Literacy Consultant, Dallas, TX